BOUNDLESS

A GUIDED PRAYER JOURNAL TO MOVE FREEDOM
FROM YOUR HEAD TO YOUR HEART

TASHA LAYTON

Copyright © 2021 Tasha Layton

All rights reserved. No part of this book may be reproduced or used in any manner without the prior written permission of the copyright owner, except for the use of brief quotations in a book review.

To request permissions, contact the publisher at info@tashalayton.com.

ISBN: 978-0-578-31620-8

First paperback edition October 2021.

Edited by Drew Tilton
Cover art and layout by Phil Earnest
Photographs | Unsplash

All Scripture quotations, unless otherwise indicated, are taken from the Holy Bible, New International Version®, NIV®. Copyright ©1973, 1978, 1984, 2011 by Biblica, Inc.™ Used by permission of Zondervan. All rights reserved worldwide. www.zondervan.com The "NIV" and "New International Version" are trademarks registered in the United States Patent and Trademark Office by Biblica, Inc.™

Scripture quotations marked (NLT) are taken from the Holy Bible, New Living Translation, copyright ©1996, 2004, 2015 by Tyndale House Foundation. Used by permission of Tyndale House Publishers, Carol Stream, Illinois 60188. All rights reserved.

Scripture quotations marked MSG are taken from THE MESSAGE, copyright © 1993, 2002, 2018 by Eugene H. Peterson. Used by permission of NavPress, represented by Tyndale House Publishers. All rights reserved.

Tasha Layton
7106 Crossroads Blvd # 215,
Brentwood, TN 37027

www.tashalayton.com

What am I doing?

The question bled from my heart as I sat sipping coffee on my parents' front porch. Overlooking the lush South Carolina greenery - boundless and free - I felt despair and frustration swirl inside me. I was stuck.

Stuck in faith. Stuck in life.

A month earlier, I had quit my job in L.A., left my church community, and moved back home. Between calling off an engagement and leaving a less than fulfilling "dream job," to say things hadn't panned out the way I had hoped was an understatement. I was thirty. No husband. No family. Little sense of my true worth.

I was determined to find a way forward, a way to experience the "abundant life" I had heard about growing up in the church, but the plans I had come up with myself hadn't materialized the full life for which I was hoping.

Now my new plan of an extended sabbatical brimming with all the "right" spiritual stuff - was working out no better. Despite my best efforts, the life I had dreamed for myself seemed endlessly out of reach. I was exhausted.

God, do I deserve this?

I didn't need Him to answer. Despite knowing in my head what the Bible declared - I am His daughter, immeasurably loved and created with purpose - a dissonance in my heart was far more convincing.

I *did* deserve this. I deserved less than what I hoped for. I deserved a bad life.

And no amount of knowledge, Bible reading, church attendance, spiritual practices, or worldly success could convince me otherwise.

Deep in the unseen parts of my heart invisible wounds weighed on me and held me back from truly accepting the things I wanted so desperately to believe. These deep unaddressed traumas unconsciously impacted the way I saw everything.

The world, myself, God. Everything.

I needed help. That much was clear. What wasn't clear in that moment was the journey God was inviting me into. A journey of discovery and budding freedom with God through a practice commonly known as *healing prayer*. That journey would

change my heart and life forever.

This is the same journey I believe God has for you. To dive deep past head-knowledge and into the depths of your own woundedness and pain with God, so He can personally offer His powerful and transformative truth in the face of the deep-seated lies you have come to unconsciously believe.

Obviously, this will not be easy, and things often seem like they get worse before getting better. But I want to encourage you by saying this painful (at times) journey with God is all worth it. I want you to know that there is a life beyond the feelings of inadequacy and self-doubt. Beyond the fears of being unlovable and less than enough.

There is hope. There is freedom.

There are real pathways to growth when we open ourselves to God and invite Him into the hidden places of our heart, allowing Him to care for us at our most vulnerable.

In this journal you will find no systematic method or magic formula. Yes, there is plenty here to learn and apply, but ultimately healing can only come from God Himself. My hope instead is that God would meet you in between these pages, that He would use my story and your prayers to facilitate in you your own journey towards freedom - a journey that lasts long after you are finished with this journal.

I pray through God's strength these are your first steps towards a life that is full, whole, and utterly boundless.

Your Friend,
Tasha

About this journal

Throughout this journal, there is a rhythm of stories, readings, prayer prompts, and engagement activities designed to help you learn about and explore a process commonly known as healing prayer.

This process that I share is hardly an original idea. As you will see, someone guided me through it, and Christians have been implementing these healing prayer practices for over a thousand years. Really, I am just sharing with you a collection of these time-tested practices and my journey with them in hopes that they will be as immensely helpful for you as they have been for me.

The first three sections of this journal are simply introducing and encouraging you to explore the various prayer practices that make up the healing prayer process.

In part one, we will look at the healing prayer process as a whole, with an eye toward understanding what healing prayer is, what it is not, and what it is seeking to address. Part two will lay out a cornerstone practice of healing prayer: inviting God to help you reimagine wounding memories. Part three will guide you through the powerful practice of rejecting the unconscious lies and vows that have grown from these wounding memories, asking God to offer reshaping truth to grow in their place.

We do not dive into prac-

ticing the full-fledged healing prayer process until the fourth and final section.

This is intentional to help you approach this process gently and with patience.

Much of what you will explore with God will be difficult and painful. That is not necessarily a bad thing, especially if you - like me - are used to stuffing emotions down rather than feeling them. That said, it is okay to take your time learning about the various elements of this process found in parts one through three and exploring them with God before beginning the final section.

Diving into the deep end (your most painful memory) right out of the gate is probably not wise. Take your time splashing in the shallows with God before moving on into greater depths. This is not a *30 Days of...* type prayer journal. I want you to commit to taking the time you need and not moving into those more difficult areas until you feel ready.

When the time is right, part four will offer you a practical scaffolding that outlines the entire process of healing prayer. Here you will finally be introduced to the **process pages** that will help to facilitate your healing **prayer process** as you intentionally surrender the wounded and guarded parts of your heart to God's transforming power.

(You can preview a sample of the full healing prayer process on the *sample process* page on the next page.)

I also want to encourage you to allow God's grace, compassion, and unconditional love to flow freely towards your heart and mind. Any time we open to God's freedom we can *expect* opposition seeking to shame us, distract us from God's love, and discourage us from continuing. Often this comes in the form of the very lies we are seeking to have God uproot. Expect this

that judging and shaming yourself is counterproductive.

Ask if the words and phrases you are hearing sound like something God would say to you. You can do this by comparing what is being said with the Biblical definition of love in 1 Corinthians 13:4-7. (i.e. Are these phrases directed towards me: patient, kind, not easily angered, keeping no record of wrongs, always protecting, trusting, hoping, persevering, etc.?) If they do not meet this criteria they are not from God. Simply recognize them as a lie and allow yourself to move on without dwelling on them. If they are important God will bring you back to them through the process of healing prayer and uproot them on your behalf.

As you explore these pages with God, keep in mind that this journal cannot (and is not intended to) replace the care of trained mental health professionals. If anything, I hope it can supplement that care. I encourage us all to consult such professionals as we work through these pages and consider inviting them into our process. Also consider inviting a trusted friend to pray for you as you journey with God. You don't have to share every aspect of your journey with them, but simply ask them to lift you up before God while you are engaging in healing prayer.

Finally, remember that God *can* - and wants to - heal, redeem, and make you whole. Sometimes it is easy to believe we are too far gone or beyond healing, but I assure you that is a lie. Allow God, who knows exactly what is best for you in every moment, to lead you to the truth your heart needs. The process laid out here is simply framework to get you started, but God may lead you off script a bit. That is okay and encouraged. Ultimately, He is the one who will *guide you into all truth.* (See Jn 16:13)

Blessings on your journey toward healing my friends. Know that my heart is with you throughout these pages as you allow God to "strengthen you with power through his Spirit in your inner being, so that Christ may dwell in your hearts through faith." (Eph 3:16-17a)

PART 1

Prayer That Heals

Pete brought me outside to a clearing. The Colorado air was crisp as the sun set over the Rockies. "Look at that sunset," he said. "Isn't it the most beautiful thing you've ever seen?" I agreed. It was a spectacular harmony of oranges and yellows. Incredible. After a moment's pause, Pete continued his thought. "And doesn't it stun you to know that God says you are even more beautiful than that?"

I was taken aback. He was referencing the verse we had talked about in our counseling session just minutes before. *"For we are God's handiwork, created in Christ Jesus to do good works, which God prepared in advance for us to do." (Eph 2:10)* The word translated *handiwork* here is the Greek word *Poiema* - where we get our English word, *poem*. The

COLOR THE SUNSET

original word carries with it the idea that of all that God has created, humanity is his crowning achievement. He called all of creation good except for us. He called us *very* good. If God were an artist, we'd be His *masterpiece*.

In that moment, something clicked into place for me.

> "When I think of those times I'm hurting, I see You, 'cause You're there too. And every pain I feel You healing, is so You'll see, my heart running free."
>
> *- Love Lifting Me*

God thinks I am more beautiful than every sunset that had ever existed. I am His crowning achievement, His pièce de résistance, His loved child. In that moment, I felt the freedom of that truth move from my head to my heart.

For days, God had been digging up the deep roots of the painful lies I believed about myself. That I wasn't enough, that I was dirty, evil, deserving of no good thing. Staring at that sunset, He was planting something new in my heart. An al-

> "Even though I walk through the darkest valley, I will fear no evil, for you are with me; your rod and your staff, they comfort me."
>
> *- Psalm 23:4*

ternative belief to take root in the newly tilled soil.

He was planting truth.

At that moment, my life changed. Not in every way. There were still more lies to uproot, new truths for Him to plant. But my outlook on life, on my identity, was carried to a whole new perspective. The moment was real. Not pretend-spiritual or created from my own strength or emotion. Just a good God offering me a good gift in real time.

After my failed sabbatical at my parents' house in South Carolina, I went searching for help. Searching for people who had felt what I was feeling and somehow found healing. I found Pete, a Christian counselor in Buena Vista, Colorado, trained in caring for people as they walk with God through a process Pete called *heart prayer*. Some similar practices are known as healing prayer.

Pete has been so instrumental in my journey of healing. I am immensely grateful he answered the call to shepherd me through

Selah

Take a quick inventory of your heart. How are you feeling about joining God on this journey into the dark valleys of your heart? Afraid? Hopeful? Skeptical? Curious? Without judgement or shame, jot down a quick prayer just being honest with God about where you are.

this process. That said, Pete would be the first to tell you that he was not the one who brought about healing in my life. It was God who met me in those mountains. It was God who breathed life into me, beckoned me to join Him on a journey into the darkest valleys of my heart, taught me to not fear the evil that hid there, and showed me how He was with me all along.

Have you ever wondered why we as human beings often feel stuck? Trapped in the same unhealthy patterns or unhelpful behaviors? Are you curious why certain situations trigger you? Make you instantly angry or overwhelmed? Have you ever felt an anxiety or depression that, no matter how hard you tried, you couldn't seem to shake?

I am writing this because I have been there. I am still there - in process that is. There is no quick fix for any of the deep wounds of the heart, and the more you are healed the more you realize you will always be in process. But I have also written this because God has brought a great degree of freedom to my heart. He

has brought about change.
Real change.

Change I never thought I'd actually experience.

Change I could not seem to bring about through my own effort. In this process my role was merely to follow

Him, to stop hoping He would heal the wounds I didn't permit Him to see or touch.

I learned the practice of allowing God into the hidden places of my heart through what is known as healing prayer or inner healing prayer. I like to think of it as merely learning to be more courageous and present with God, more intentional with what parts of our hearts we offer Him.

Boundless is simply meant to facilitate this journey with God in *your* life, helping you engage with Him through the time - tested practices of healing prayer - to set you on a path towards a more robust and intentional prayer life with your Creator.

The Wounds We Live From

Jesus says, "A good person produces good things from the treasury of a good heart." (Lk 6:45a, NLT) He says the opposite is true of an evil person. When you hear Jesus referring to the heart, He is talking about a person's core belief-center, "the fountain and seat of the thoughts, passions, desires, appetites, affections, purposes, endeavors."[1] His point then is not that people are inherently good or evil, but that the way we live flows from the deep-seated beliefs that we hold in our unconscious.

In the chart on this page, you can see these beliefs are shaped in our hearts from experiences throughout life, though childhood experiences are often the most powerful. They do not normally exist as neat sentences or phrases in our minds, but as feelings, intuitions, and senses about ourselves and the world around us. When we are wounded by an impactful experience, a misbelief or lie can form in our hearts.

From these deep-seated lies, commit-

- THE **WOUNDING EXPERIENCE** SHAPES A CORE MISBELIEF OR LIE
- THE **DEEP-SEATED LIE** CAUSES US TO FORM A COMMITMENT OR VOW
- THIS **VOW** SHAPES THE WAY WE SEE, EXPERIENCE, AND INTERACT WITH THE WORLD
- **LIVING THIS WAY** COSTS US TRUE FREEDOM TO LIVE AS WE WERE INTENDED

---

[1] "Kardia Meaning in Bible - New Testament Greek Lexicon - King James Version," biblestudytools.com, accessed July 16, 2021, https://www.biblestudytools.com/lexicons/greek/kjv/kardia.html. Greek lexicon based on Thayer's and Smith's Bible Dictionary plus others; this is keyed to the large Kittel and the "Theological Dictionary of the New Testament."

ments or vows form to help us cope with the misbelief and the pain we feel beneath it. These vows often reveal themselves as "I will never..." or "I will always..." statements. These vows trigger in us emotions, thoughts, and actions that flow so naturally into our lives we most often do not even realize where they came from. In short, living from our unconscious vows leads us to think and act in ways that leave us wondering, *why did I react that way? Or, why did I just do that?* The writer of the book of Romans, a man of God named Paul, explains it this way,

So I find this law at work: Although I want to do good, evil is right there with me. For in my inner being I delight in God's law; but I see another law at work in me, waging war against the law of my mind and making me a prisoner of the law of sin at work within me. (Romans 7:21-23)

Paul comments that though in his inner being he wants to follow *God's law* - or the ways of living that lead to a more flourishing and full life - there is a different law that wars deep inside of him. The word translated *at work in me* carries with it the idea of this different law being woven into the very fabric of Paul's being.[2] He identifies this internal tendency

---

[2] See "Melos Meaning in Bible - New Testament Greek Lexicon - King James Version," biblestudytools.com, accessed September 8, 2021, https://www.biblestudytools.com/lexicons/greek/kjv/melos.html. Greek lexicon based on Thayer's and Smith's Bible Dictionary plus others; this is keyed to the large Kittel and the "Theological Dictionary of the New Testament."

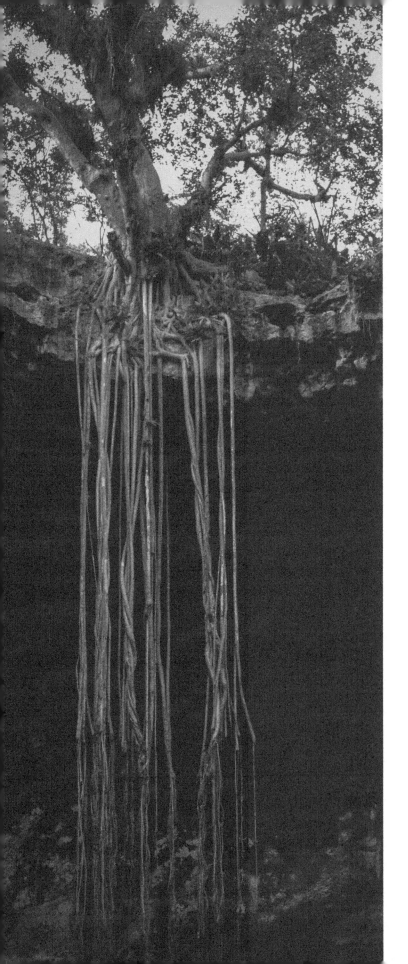

against choosing what is right as the *law of sin* - or the ways of living that lead towards death and destruction.

Paul is tapping into a deep truth about human decision making and behavioral habituation. So much of our thinking and decisions are not controlled in our conscious mind, but through subconscious belief and regularly reinforced patterns of thinking and behaving that are deeply ingrained in us.

Through Jesus we are *made new* (more on that later), but there are still residual beliefs and patterns of thinking and acting that linger in the depths of our heart. As a result, we often find ourselves living out of these instinctual beliefs and habituations, feeling helpless to live differently. We try and try to change our behavior but find ourselves drawn back to it so easily. By living from our woundedness, we lose our freedom to live as we intended.

Let me give you an example of what this looks like:

Tasha's Journal

I walked into my first-grade classroom excited for what the school day held. The scent of pencil shavings and fresh rubbed erasers filled the air, as our teacher informed us that each student would have to read aloud in front of the class that day.

As my turn approached, I realized that all the water I had that morning was catching up with me. I immediately raised my hand to ask for permission to use the little girls' room. We had a restroom right there in class and I was confident I would be back in time for my turn.

To my surprise, the teacher responded to my request with a firm "No." She told me it wasn't okay for me to try and get out of reading in front of the class. As time went on, I repeated my request three more times, unfortunately receiving the same response.

When my turn to read finally came, I was about ready to burst. I rose from my chair carefully and took my place in front of the class. As soon as I opened my mouth to read, the sensation overwhelmed me and I wet my pants in front of the whole class. I was mortified as all of my peers began to laugh.

I expected this dreadful situation to elicit compassion from my teacher. It did not. Infuriated, she sent me to the restroom in the back of the classroom, telling me to wait there. I raced into the tiny room and closed the door. I sat on the floor against the wall and waited in my shame and embarrassment.
I waited... And waited... And waited some more.

Hours went by and I realized my teacher had no intention of coming to retrieve me. She left me in the restroom the entire day. When I got home from school, I found prank messages on my answering machine from some of the other kids in the class. Even years later I could not think of this experience without feeling deep shame.

As an adult,

I rarely thought of this situation other than the infrequent occasions my friends and I would swap embarrassing childhood stories. I figured all kids get teased, so why couldn't I just get over it? I had no idea the impact that experience had on the way I saw myself.

Through healing prayer I realized that that wounding experience caused me to believe the lie: *I am dirty, shameful, and something is wrong with me.* Though I did not realize it until decades later, from that day on I lived from that lie vowing to *never let anyone see the real me.*

So, I performed, became hyper driven to accomplish great things. I worked hard to be liked and never give anyone a reason to reject me. It was like I was still that little girl hiding in the bathroom, too ashamed to let anyone see how dirty I am.

Because I believed something was wrong with me, I didn't think I deserved anything good in life. I saw the bad things in my life as proof of this and habituated myself to sabotage the good parts of my life.

That day in the first grade, I lost my freedom to be the real me, and no external remedy was going to change that. Not success, not church, not even learning and embracing Biblical truth in my conscious mind. I was attempting to repair something deeply internal (my habituated heart) with things that were inherently external (my actions and conscious thoughts).

This led me to try to address with mere will - power a misbelief and vow that had been reinforced over and over again throughout my life. This is why I found such minimal effectiveness in changing these deeply rooted and habituated problems with my own internal strength.

I was like a hamster in a wheel, running furiously yet going nowhere - exhausted.

Immediately following Paul's teaching in Romans 7:21-23, he writes what I was feeling deep in my heart, while also revealing my only hope for change.

> *What a wretched man I am! Who will rescue me from this body that is subject to death? Thanks be to God, who delivers me through Jesus Christ our Lord!*

I needed God to take me back into the memory of my wounding experience and deliver me from my misbeliefs and habituations.

I needed to allow Him to do what only He could do.

Heal.

Though the mountains may be moved into the sea, Though the ground beneath might crumble and give way, I can hear my Father singing over me, "It's gonna be ok, it's gonna be ok"

- Into the Sea

Selah

What stands out to you about this section? What do you sense God might be saying to you? How does Jesus' teaching in Luke 6:45a ("A good person produces good things from the treasury of a good heart." - NLT) make you think differently about the heart? How might God be leading you in this early stage of the process?

A Prayer of Protection

Before moving on in this process, would you consider engaging with God through this prayer of protection? Our spiritual enemy does not want us to experience freedom, and we should expect opposition. I encourage you to pray the following prayer aloud with God and return to it as often as you need. I recommend opening with this prayer each time you engage with God through this journal.

God, I commit this time to You. I ask for Your protection over me and over my family and friends. Lead me through this process and come alongside me through Your Holy Spirit. Show me the lies You want to dig up and what parts of my heart You want to heal. Help me to have the courage to follow You, even when it feels uncomfortable. Thank You for Your healing and what You will do in me through this process. I love You and pray to You in the name of Jesus. Amen.

Write a Letter

Write a letter to God telling Him about what you hope engaging with Him through this journal might bring. Be honest with Him about your feelings around your healing journey and any fears you may have (e.g., this won't work, I can't really experience freedom, etc.).

Our Emotions Have Something to Say

Though not always reflective of what is true about us or a situation, our emotions are a very real experience internally. Emotions operate as signal lights, drawing our attention to what is going on in our internal world. Often it is tempting to avoid, stuff down, or distract ourselves from our emotions, but this is detrimental to our spiritual and mental health in the long run. Throughout this journal, you will be asked to engage with your emotions for the sake of identifying what they have to say.

Using the chart on the next page, practice identifying the emotions you have felt over the past week. In the sections provided, write out what those emotions might be trying to tell you.

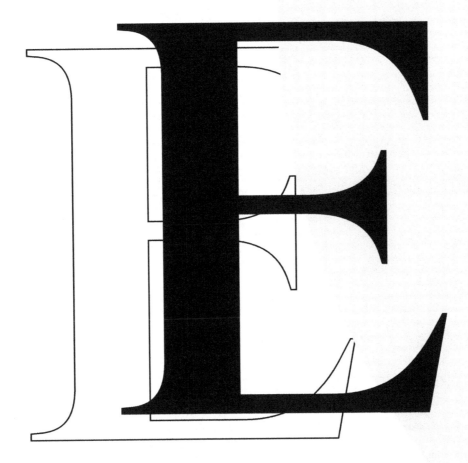

Emotion Wheel

Core emotions (center): ANGER, SHAME, SAD, HAPPY, SURPRISE, FEAR

ANGER
- MAD: ENRAGED, FURIOUS, VIOLATED, RESENTFUL, JEALOUS
- HATEFUL: HOSTILE, PROVOKED
- AGGRESSIVE: INFURIATED, IRRITATED
- FRUSTRATED: WITHDRAWN, SUSPICIOUS
- DISTANT: SKEPTICAL, SARCASTIC
- CRITICAL: JUDGMENTAL, LOATHING

SHAME
- DISAPPROVAL: REPUGNANT, REVOLTED
- DISAPPOINTED: REVULSION, DETESTABLE
- AWFUL: AVERSION, HESITANT
- AVOIDANCE: REMORSEFUL
- GUILTY: ASHAMED

SAD
- ABANDONED: IGNORED, VICTIMIZED
- DESPAIR: POWERLESS
- DEPRESSED: VULNERABLE
- LONELY: INFERIOR, EMPTY
- BORED: ABANDONED, ISOLATED
- OPTIMISTIC: APATHETIC, INDIFFERENT

HAPPY
- INTIMATE: INSPIRED, OPEN
- PEACEFUL: PLAYFUL, SENSITIVE
- POWERFUL: HOPEFUL, LOVING
- ACCEPTED: PROVOCATIVE, COURAGEOUS
- PROUD: RESPECTED, FULFILLED
- INTERESTED: IMPORTANT, CONFIDENT

SURPRISE
- JOYFUL: AMUSED, INQUISITIVE
- EXCITED: ECSTATIC, LIBERATED
- AMAZED: ENERGETIC, EAGER
- CONFUSED: AWE
- STARTLED: ASTONISHED, PERPLEXED
- SCARED: DISILLUSIONED, DISMAYED

FEAR
- ANXIOUS: SHOCKED, TERRIFIED
- INSECURE: FRIGHTENED, OVERWHELMED
- SUBMISSIVE: WORRIED, INADEQUATE
- REJECTED: INFERIOR, WORTHLESS
- HUMILIATED: INSIGNIFICANT, INADEQUATE
- HURT: ALIENATED, DISRESPECTED
- THREATENED: RIDICULED, EMBARRASSED, DEVASTATED

Emotion

What this emotion is telling you

You may also use these pages to fill in emotions as they come to you at a later time to help process.

Emotion

What this emotion is telling you

You may also use these pages to fill in emotions as they come to you at a later time to help process.

Emotion

What this emotion is telling you

You may also use these pages to fill in emotions as they come to you at a later time to help process.

Emotion

What this emotion is telling you

You may also use these pages to fill in emotions as they come to you at a later time to help process.

Emotion

What this emotion is telling you

You may also use these pages to fill in emotions as they come to you at a later time to help process.

Emotion

What this emotion is telling you

You may also use these pages to fill in emotions as they come to you at a later time to help process.

Emotion

What this emotion is telling you

You may also use these pages to fill in emotions as they come to you at a later time to help process.

Emotion

What this emotion is telling you

You may also use these pages to fill in emotions as they come to you at a later time to help process.

Emotion

What this emotion is telling you

You may also use these pages to fill in emotions as they come to you at a later time to help process.

Inviting God into our Memories Through Healing Prayer

In the Colorado counseling room, Pete walked me through the memory of wetting my pants in front of my first-grade classroom.

He encouraged me to describe the memory in detail. What happened? How did you feel? How did others respond?

I talked through the painful experience.
"What hurt most?" he compassionately asked. "What did you lose?" I looked at my shoes, nervous and ashamed, as though I was that six-year-old again. I told him about losing the real me, losing my freedom.

He asked me about the lie I believed. I reported tearfully: *I am dirty, shameful, something is wrong with me, I deserve the bad things that have happened to me.* I told him about the vow to not let anyone see me, not really.

Next is where things got... different.

"And when you pray, do not be like the hypocrites, for they love to pray standing in the synagogues and on the street corners to be seen by others. Truly I tell you, they have received their reward in full. But when you pray, go into your room, close the door and pray to your Father, who is unseen. Then your Father, who sees what is done in secret, will reward you. And when you pray, do not keep on babbling like pagans, for they think they will be heard because of their many words. Do not be like them, for your Father knows what you need before you ask him.

- *(Mt 6:5-8)*

"Now, I want you to invite God to take control of and speak to you through your imagination," Pete said, confident and caring. "I want you to go back with Him to that day in first grade, to imagine you are there experiencing it all over again."

I did as Pete asked, tentatively offering my imagination to be a tool for God to speak.

"Where are you right now?" Pete asked gently.

"I'm in the bathroom sitting on the floor, my knees to my chest."
"How do you feel?"

"Just... dirty. I feel dirty. And ashamed." The emotions from that day bubbled in my chest.

"And Jesus, do you see Jesus? Where is He in the picture?"

I did see Him, strong and robed, in front of me between me and the toilet. He was sitting on the floor like me with His legs crossed.

"What does Jesus want to say to you right now?" Pete asked.

Jesus didn't say anything. Instead, He scooped me up into His arms and sat me on His lap. He wasn't ashamed of me, nor did He think I was dirty. It didn't even matter that

I had soiled my pants. He held me in His arms as though I was His child.

I knew in that moment with Jesus, tears streaming down my face, that I was not deserving of all the bad that had come my way. I knew with Jesus I was innocent.

I only fully understood the way Jesus saw me that day years later. I reflected on the innocence I see in my own children, considering how I would respond with compassion and care if they were in my situation.

This is an example of what healing prayer looked like for me. Though no time in prayer is ever the same, there are basic questions you can walk yourself through with God that will help you open to what He wants to do in your life.

It is helpful to remember that prayer is simply connecting with God in relationship. In Matthew 5 Jesus tells His followers,

> *"And when you pray, do not be like the hypocrites, for they love to pray standing in the synagogues and on the street corners to be seen by others. Truly I tell you, they have received their reward in full. But when you pray, go into your room, close the door and pray to your Father, who is unseen. Then your Father, who sees what is done in secret, will reward you. And when you pray, do not keep*

on babbling like pagans, for they think they will be heard because of their many words. Do not be like them, for your Father knows what you need before you ask him. (Mt 6:5-8)

Jesus assures us that we do not need to have the right words to say or even to say anything. If God knows what we need, then we can be assured that prayer is first and foremost about our relationship with Him.

Healing prayer then is connecting in relationship with God for the sake of healing our inner selves.

Over the course of this journal we will be exploring in more detail the various elements of healing prayer, but remember, the power is not in the practices themselves or doing things exactly the right way.

True healing only comes when we allow God to join us in the difficult places of our hearts.

Also, keep in mind that this is a process. Every human heart is a tangled mess of roots and lies that take time to sort through and offer to God. We will never be perfect. But with time and God's loving presence in our hearts, we will find far greater levels of freedom than we previously thought possible.

Yourself through Jesus' Eyes

Draw a portrait of yourself the way a loving God would see you. This is not about being a good artist. Use words or symbolism to represent what you think God loves about you.

Selah

What stands out to you about this section? What do you think of the idea of God using your imagination to speak to you? Tell Him honestly how you feel about the idea.

Picturing the Future

Draw two pictures in the space provided. First draw something that depicts where you are right now in relation to feeling inwardly free. Next to it draw something that depicts where you hope to be in relation to feeling inwardly free. Afterwards spend some time journaling to God about what you notice in your drawings. This is not about being a good artist but about expressing to God and yourself your feelings and hopes.

Timeline Exersize

In the space provided, use the sections of the page to represent five-year increments[1] of your life (i.e., 1-5 years old, 6-10 years old, and so on). In each section record the things that stand out to you about that era. Consider key events, people, and situations that impacted you - positively, negatively, or neutral. Alternatively, you can draw a picture in each section to represent that era of your life. Take as long as you need and feel free to use all of the next few pages. We will be returning to this timeline regularly throughout this process. If more space is needed, consider using a separate notebook or sheets of paper.

---

[1] You may also consider dividing your timeline into five-year increments for your childhood and then shifting to 10 year increments for your old adulthood.

A G E S : _____ - _____

A G E S : _____ - _____

A G E S : _____ - _____

A G E S : _____ - _____

A G E S : _____ - _____

A G E S : _____ - _____

A G E S : _____ - _____

A G E S : _____ - _____

A G E S : _____ - _____

AGES: _____ - _____

AGES: _____ - _____

AGES: _____ - _____

A G E S : _____ - _____

A G E S : _____ - _____

A G E S : _____ - _____

A G E S : _____ - _____

A G E S : _____ - _____

A G E S : _____ - _____

Child-Like Faith

Schedule some time this week to do something that you loved to do as a kid. Paint, dance, go to a park, set up a game of tag, play with Legos, or buy an ice cream cone. Invite God to accompany you on this adventure. Afterwards reflect on the time in the space below.

"But Jesus said, "Let the children come to me. Don't stop them! For the Kingdom of Heaven belongs to those who are like these children."

Matthew 19:14, NLT

PART 2
RE-IMAGINING WITH GOD

As I began the process of exploring the roots of my *stuck-ness* with my counselor Pete, God started to bring to my attention painful memories from my past.

I was shocked by the power of one memory in particular, and the impact it continued to have on the way I lived my entire life up to that point. It wasn't even a memory of something that actually happened, but of a vivid and terrifying nightmare I once had as a very young girl.

Yet, as a thirty-year-old sitting across from Pete, fear and shame flowed powerfully through my body as I recounted to him the details of the dream - details I will spare you of. What is important is that the dream involved me being subjected to a dark and deeply twisted trauma.

I had never shared this nightmare with anyone. I thought this was because it was insignificant. It was "normal." Kids have nightmares. They get over it and move on.

I have learned, however, it is not so much the experience itself that imprints us, but our interpretation and response to that experience. In his book, *What Happened to You?*, Dr. Bruce Perry uses the example of a fire at an elementary school. A firefighter and a first grader both experience the same event, but in radically different ways. Where the fire is routine and somewhat mundane for the firefighter, the first

grader is deeply terrified by the incident. He goes on to write,

This illustrates one of the key issues in understanding a potentially traumatic event: How does the *individual* experience the event? What is going on inside the person; is the stress response activated in extreme or prolonged ways... Any long-term effects are related to several factors, including the nature of your stress response... as well as the intensity and pattern of that response.[1]

This is an important point when it comes to exploring our own trauma. Events that we might assume to be insignificant can traumatize us greatly if our minds - especially as children - experience the danger as real and our stress response is activated at a high level.

This is the difference between

---
[1] Perry, Bruce D., and Oprah Winfrey. What Happened to You?: Conversations on Trauma, Resilience, and Healing. New York, NY: Flatiron Books, 2021.

what is real and what is *reality*.

Clearly the trauma my five-year-old brain experienced through that nightmare, along with the deep-seated belief it shaped in my heart, were real.

I *really* felt terrified and ashamed. I *really* believed that I was evil. I believed that anyone who could dream up something so dark and twisted, must themselves be dark and twisted.

But that does not mean these emotions and beliefs reflect *reality*. When I step outside of myself and assess what happened as a rational adult, I know there can be any number of reasons for my having that dream. I can also see clearly that my experience and the conclusion I came to, though very real to me at the time, did not reflect reality as it actually was.

Yet at the time, I was too young to offer an alternative explanation to myself and too ashamed to share it with anyone who could correct it. Instead, I buried this memory and the lie that sprouted from it. As a result, this lie - hidden in my subconscious - dug its roots deep into my heart.

You see, what we believe on the deepest level impacts all our decision making even when we do not realize it.

Because I believed I was evil, I vowed to never let anyone see this darkness that lived in me. Like a muscle, the roots of the lie grew stronger and stronger - and I became more and more habituated - the more I lived from it. No matter how much evidence there was to the contrary throughout my life, the misbelief persisted, and with it the fear of being "found out." I interpreted bad things in life as being a result of my evil, and my achievement-oriented way of living reinforced and perpetuated the lie all the further.

Of course, I was not consciously aware of any of this. Not until Jesus helped me confront the memory from where this trauma was birthed.

The Impact of Traumatic Memories

You see, our memories are powerful. Like, really powerful. Memories and the experiences they come from can cause trauma. Trauma is deep and lasting psycho-emotional pain that comes from our perception of a given experience or collection of experiences. Trauma can be self-inflicted, inflicted by another person, or inflicted by an event.

We often rush to write off even the most clearly traumatic memories of our past as inconsequential to our lives today. But the more we learn, the more we realize their real and lasting impact. Trauma expert Dr. Bessel van der Kolk writes,

We have learned that trauma is not just an event that took place sometime in the past; it is also the imprint left by that experience on mind, brain, and body. This imprint has ongoing consequences for how the human organism manages to survive in the present. Trauma results in a fundamental reorganization of the way mind and brain manage perceptions. It changes not only how we think and what we think about, but also our very capacity to think.[1]

Apparently, trauma shifts our entire perception of reality, impacting the way we think about and interact with the world. This

---
1 Van der Kolk, Bessel. The Body Keeps the Score: Brain, Mind, and Body in the Healing of Trauma. New York, NY: Penguin Books, 2015.

does not mean these beliefs reflect reality as it actually is, but what we believe about reality.

As is often the case, we are re-affirming with science what is clearly revealed in scripture. We can't even make it past the first book of the Bible without seeing a clear pattern of trauma and its impact on the way we as humans live. The tragic and painful family stories of Genesis are perfect case studies on the impact of trauma.

We read about God's original intention for creation in Genesis

> I rub my eyes cuz I am trying to find a reason,
> Why nothing changes and I'm stuck in this season.
>
> *-I Got You*

1 and 2, about the first man and woman who lived with God in Eden. In Eden, humanity would understand that they - and each human being with them - are made in the image of God and deserving of incredible honor and love.

They would see themselves and each other as beautiful, able to

60

exist naked - fully exposed - yet feel no shame. Humanity would walk side-by-side with God, understanding Him as a loving, good, and powerful creator.

Unfortunately, in Genesis 3 we also read about humanity's rejection of God, in favor of a lie.

We will explore this lie and humanity's original rejection of God in the next section, but for now just know the world was thrown into incredible chaos almost immediately.

We are talking death, destruction, loss, murder, infertility, slavery, rape, incest, betrayal, polygamy, human-trafficking, and war all before we even get to Moses.

The good news is that we also see all throughout Genesis (and scripture for that matter) a God that is continually restoring, redeeming, and healing the traumas of those who offer these wounds to Him. In a very real way, God's redeeming journey in each of our lives and hearts - and in the world as a whole - is Him lovingly bringing us back to His original intention for creation. He wants to again walk among us, teach us who we really are and who He really is.

He wants to bring us back to Eden. The story of Joseph is a great example. (See Gen 37-50)

Joseph's family situation was messy and rife with trauma. Joseph was one of twelve brothers, born of four different mothers from their father Jacob (also known as Israel). Jacob had two wives, Leah and Rachel, who were also sisters. Jacob only really loved Rachel, the younger sister, and treated Leah poorly throughout their marriage. Rachel, the mother of Joseph, died in childbirth of her second son Benjamin. Jacob also conceived with two of his wives' servants, Bilhah and Zilpah.

> Even at my worst, you gave me Your best And when my heart was hurt, you loved me to death.
>
> *- I Belong To You*

For obvious reasons Jacob's twelve sons had many issues and were pitted against each other much of their lives. To further complicate things, Jacob

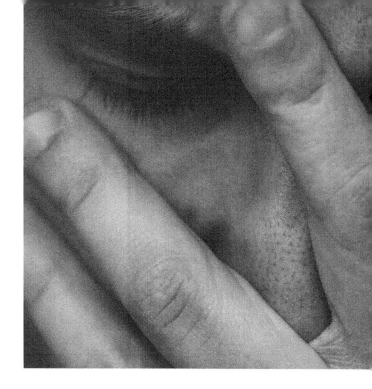

"loved Joseph more than any of his other sons, because he had been born to him in his old age; and he made an ornate robe for him. When his brothers saw that their father loved him more than any of them, they hated him and could not speak a kind word to him." (Gen 37:3-4)

Joseph lived out of this unhealth and treated his brothers with little respect, acting arrogantly around them. Eventually, the trauma of this tumultuous family situation boiled over, as a group of Joseph's brothers sold him into slavery.

Joseph was taken to Egypt as a

slave and faced trauma after trauma. Yet, in the midst of his struggles, Joseph turned to God again and again, and God brought about good for Joseph despite, and even from, his difficulty. Eventually Joseph found himself serving at the highest level in Egypt, elevated to the chief authority second only to the Pharaoh.

Years later, a famine brings Joseph's brothers (all but Rachel's other son Benjamin) to Egypt to purchase grain from their storehouses - storehouses that God instructed Joseph to create so that many lives would be saved. Though they do not recognize Joseph, Joseph recognizes them. You can feel Joseph's anger in the passages, as the memories of his traumas undoubtedly rush back to him. Living from that anger, the formerly enslaved man falsely accuses his brothers of being spies and imprisons them. He eventually agrees to allow all but one of the brothers go home if they bring Benjamin, whom he loves, back to Egypt.

The story comes to a climax when all of Joseph's brothers are before him and he reveals his true identity,
Then Joseph could no longer control himself before all his at-

tendants, and he cried out, "Have everyone leave my presence!" So there was no one with Joseph when he made himself known to his brothers. And he wept so loudly that the Egyptians heard him, and Pharaoh's household heard about it. (Gen 45:1-2)

In this moment Joseph's heart is cracked open and the pain of his traumatic memories spills out for all to see. But rather than seeking further revenge, God works in Joseph's heart helping him to heal from his wounds and eventually forgive his brothers.

This culminates in Joseph saying of his brothers' actions, "You intended to harm me, but God intended it for good to accomplish what is now being done, the saving of many lives." (Gen 50:20) Though God didn't necessarily cause Joseph's trauma, He used it to ultimately bring about good for Joseph and many others.

When we are faced with traumatic experiences, it is easy to struggle with questions about God's goodness, love, and power. I have found myself asking questions like: *If He is really so good, how could He ever let these awful things happen to me?*

It seemed to me that either God must not be that good, not really love me, or not be all that powerful. I even found myself questioning if He exists at all. While we won't try to answer these difficult questions here, Joseph's words reveal a powerful truth.

Though we are inflicted harm by ourselves and others, the immense power of God's redeeming love in our lives is strong enough to overcome that wounding and bring about good. In fact, God sees the cycle of trauma started by humanity's original rejection of Him and it pains Him deeply.

So much so that He has put into action a plan that will restore everything back to Eden and the way He always intended it to be.

But more on that later.

For now, let us see that this restoration to Eden extends to you and me - to our traumatic memories and the wounds they cause us.

In this section, we will be walking through a vital element of healing prayer, the practice of reimagination. We will be using prayer to explore memories with God as He speaks to us through our imagination. By inviting God into our memories and the trauma they seed, we allow God to confront and correct our misbelief at its genesis. In doing so, we give Him permission to take what was intended for harm in our lives and use it for good.

In this, God shows us His goodness, power and love for us. In this, He begins to restore us to freedom.

Selah

How do you sense God leading you as you read about the lasting impact our memories have on us? What might God be highlighting for you in the above section?

"And we know that in all things God works for the good of those who love him, who have been called according to his purpose."

Romans 8:28

Circling Back to Your Timeline

Spend some time prayerfully looking at the timeline you created in the last section. Ask God if there are any memories He would like to highlight for you. Without diving into the reimagining process now, simply tell God how you are feeling about potentially re-engaging with these memories, remembering that your experience of emotion is real and can be a window into the hidden areas of your heart. Consider referring to the emotion wheel in the previous section to help you identify what you might be feeling. Record your prayer in the journaling space below.

Connecting with Your Body

We often forget that as human beings our bodies are deeply connected with our minds and spirits. As a result, our anxieties and traumas can manifest physically. In the body below, shade in the places where you are carrying your anxiety right now (or where you normally carry your anxiety). Then close your eyes and focus on that area of your body, taking slow deep breaths with God. As you do, ask Him if He would relieve some of the tension you are experiencing, replacing it with His peace

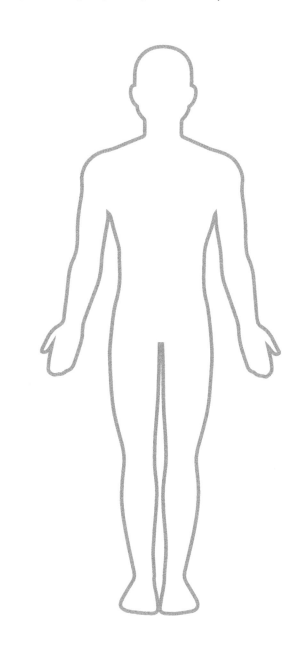

Humanity's cycle of trauma has continued from the days of Genesis, impacting generation after generation, all the way up to the present. No one has come out unscathed, and each of us has had our understandings of ourselves, God, and the world around us skewed by the pains of our past. For me, the trauma of my dream led me to misunderstand who I was, how others saw me, and how God saw me. Using the practice of reimagination, God was able to meet me at the root of those misbeliefs and reshape them inside of me.

The Practice of Reimagination

"Hey," He continues, lovingly drawing my gaze to His smile that somehow brightens the room, "you can always talk to me about how you are feeling. You don't have to prove to me that you are good. I already know that because I made you."

Tasha's Journal

I imagine myself as the five-year-old who experienced that traumatic dream. I am now awake in my childhood bed, but the wake of the almost tangible nightmare has left me overwhelmed and sobbing uncontrollably. I feel alone. The pitch black of my room reflects the heavy darkness I feel inside of me - my hidden evil that undoubtedly manifested that awful nightmare. I am terrified and ashamed.

My counselor Pete's voice brings calm to my heart, reminding me that this is a memory, a reimagination. "Where is Jesus, Tasha?" he asks gently. I inhale deeply through my nose to slow my breathing. With my mind's-eye, I search the darkness of my childhood bedroom for Jesus.

I see Him, or feel Him, rather. He is next to me sitting on my bed. He wraps his arm around my small shaking body and a wave of peace sweeps over me.

"But Jesus," I ask with my little girl voice, "what about the darkness inside me?"

"You know, Tash," He says affectionately, "there is evil in this world and I am taking care of it. But that really has nothing to do with you or this dream you had." In that moment, I feel Jesus ever so gently confronting the lie in me - that I am evil.

I realize just how much I've allowed this trauma to rule over my entire life. How I have tried to prove to absolutely everyone that I am good and not evil. His simple words bring such comfort to my young heart, as he speaks to me there in my imagination.

In this example, Jesus helps me to realign my beliefs with the truth through the practice of reimaginative prayer. This practice of allowing God to restore our understanding of reality is rooted in deep biblical truth.

One of the major focuses of the New Testament is helping humanity embrace our restored identity as sons and daughters of God through the saving work of Jesus. (See Jn 1:12, Rom 8:16, 2 Cor 6:18, Gal 3:26, etc.) As I alluded to in the previous section, God came through Jesus to our world that humanity and everything else with it would be restored to the original intention. (See Acts 3:21)

That includes me and that includes you.

God wants us to again be close with Him, like it was in Eden. To have nothing standing in between us and Him.

Though through trust in Jesus we are made right with God instantly, God is also interested in helping to reshape our skewed perception of reality caused by our traumas - what we believe about ourselves, God, and the world around us - so that we can live life

> But to all who believed him and accepted him, he gave the right to become children of God.
>
> *- John 1:12*

more fully with Him.

Take Ephesians 3 for example. In his letter, the Apostle Paul writes:

> I pray that out of his glorious riches he may strengthen you with power through his Spirit in your inner being, so that Christ may dwell in your hearts through faith. And I pray that you, being rooted and established in love, may have power, together with all the Lord's holy people, to grasp how wide and long and high and deep is the love of Christ, and to know this love that surpasses knowledge - that you may be filled to the measure of all the fullness of God. (Eph 3:16-19)

It seems that God is interested in forming our inner selves (or hearts) so they can better accept Him in His fullness. The word *grasp* in this passage carries with it the idea of taking full possession of the understanding of His unfathomable love for us.[1] We get the sense then that God strengthens us internally through reshaping our deepest understanding of reality. As this process works its way through our core beliefs, we are able to allow God to fill the hidden places of our hearts more and more.

Another helpful passage in understanding how God shapes us is Romans 12:2, which says, "Do not conform to the pattern of this world, but be transformed" by the renewing of your mind. Then you will be able to test and approve what God's will is - his good, pleasing and perfect will."

Notice that the verse says be transformed. This is not something we do ourselves, but rather a process of growth God wants to guide us through. *He transforms*

---

1 See "Katalambano Meaning in Bible - New Testament Greek Lexicon - King James Version," biblestudytools.com, accessed July 29, 2021, https://www.biblestudytools.com/lexicons/greek/kjv/katalambano.html. Greek lexicon based on Thayer's and Smith's Bible Dictionary plus others; this is keyed to the large Kittel and the "Theological Dictionary of the New Testament."

us by *the renewing of our minds*. The word mind here means, "the faculties of perceiving and understanding and those of feeling, judging, determining... of recognizing goodness and of hating evil"[2]

> Standing in your presence, Lord, I can feel you diggin' all the roots up. I feel ya healin' all my wounds up. All I can say is hallelujah.
>
> *- Look What You've Done*

In other words, He wants to restore our deepest perception of reality back to the truth. In this we will be able to *test and approve* - recognize - what is good (His truth about us, Himself, and the world), what is evil (the lies we believe about ourselves, God, and the world), and be able to live from that truth instead.

The practice of reimagination with God is powerful, yet it is only one aspect of healing prayer. In the sections that follow we will be exploring more closely how to identify the lies we believe and the vows we live by, as well as what it looks like to embrace God's truth for you and the full life of freedom He desires to share with you.

In the last section you will be bringing the entire healing prayer process together. Until then, I encourage you to take your time and be patient with yourself as you allow God to gently and powerfully lead you in this process of removing the roots of pain as He *renews your mind*.

---

[2] "Nous Meaning in Bible - New Testament Greek Lexicon - King James Version," biblestudytools.com, accessed July 28, 2021, https://www.biblestudytools.com/lexicons/greek/kjv/nous.html. Greek lexicon based on Thayer's and Smith's Bible Dictionary plus others; this is keyed to the large Kittel and the "Theological Dictionary of the New Testament."

Selah

What reservations do you have about reimagining trauma with God? Spend time just being honest with God about where you are and what you are feeling.

"I will give you a new heart and put a new spirit in you; I will remove from you your heart of stone and give you a heart of flesh."

- Ezekiel 36:26

In My Own Words

Using Paul's prayer adapted from Ephesians, spend some time rewriting the prayer of strengthening line by line in your own words. Do not get too hung up on doing this right, but rather offer your genuine hopes of growth up to God.

I pray that out of your glorious riches...

You may strengthen me with power through your Spirit in my inner being...

so that Christ may dwell in my heart through faith...

And that I, being rooted and established in love...

may have power, together with all the Lord's holy people...

to grasp how wide and long and high and deep is your love Christ...

and to know this love that surpasses knowledge...

that I may be filled to the measure of all the fullness of You, God.

Adapted from Eph 3:16-19, NIV

Practicing Reimagination with God

Spend some time in prayer asking God if there is a memory that you and He could practice reimagining together. I recommend not rushing immediately into the most painful memory you have, but choosing one that you can simply practice reimagination with God at an entry level. It can even be a positive memory to start. Picture yourself in the memory (the sights, smells, sounds, emotions, etc.) and ask God where Jesus is in the memory. In your imagination ask Jesus if He has anything He wants to say to you in that memory. When you are done, draw a picture of the moment with Jesus below. Don't worry about being a good artist or getting every detail right. It is simply a way to engage with Jesus by using a different part of your brain. When we can move trauma from our memories from the section of our brain that controls "fight, flight, or freeze," we can further the healing process.

Sights, smells, sounds, etc. of memory:

Emotions surrounding the memory:

Describe where Jesus is in this memory:

Jesus, what do you want to say to me?

Draw a picture of the moment with Jesus below:

Get Active

Doing something active or tangible can be a huge stress relief. Set a time in your calendar to do something active or tangible, just you and God. Go for a walk, make a meal, enjoy a spa day. What is important is that you allow yourself a breather from the heaviness of your memories and just enjoy time with God, who loves you. Journal about your experience in the space provided.

PART 3
CONFRONTING LIES AND VOWS

Full disclosure, I put this part of my story later in this journal because of how potentially triggering it is. There is no need to feel like you have to read this section all in one sitting. Give yourself permission to take it in pieces if needed, feeling free to go for a walk, take some deep breaths, or call a trusted friend.

Tasha's Journal

I lift the gun from its hiding place in the desk drawer. The weight of the cool metal is familiar in my twenty-year-old hand. Placing it carefully in front of me, the pistol taps against the desk's surface almost imperceptibly - the only noise filling the electric air of my college dorm room.

Through the high arching windows, afternoon warmth spills into the unconventionally beautiful dormitory with its hardwood floor and vaulted ceiling. I look out at the immaculately maintained landscape of the college campus - the peaceful setting a dissonant chord in an otherwise dark moment.

Sitting with my gun in front of me like this has become a ritual - just in case I want to follow through one day. In this moment, I feel a surge of adrenaline affirm my decision.
No more rehearsals.

Today I will end my life.

The internal barrage of accusations I hear today are nothing new: You are worthless; No one will miss you; You are so alone; They all hate you anyway; They will be better off. However, the turmoil and torment of the months leading up to this moment have left me weak, isolated and hopeless.

My senior year of high school had started off well enough. I enjoyed all things creative and was involved heavily in the arts. I was a leader in my church youth group, a part of the worship team, and was living the "model" Christian life. I never drank, never partied, never did drugs, never cursed, and never had sex - partially a relentless effort to prove to myself and others that I was not as evil as I felt.

Although many lies had already taken root in my heart, they were well hidden up to this point. As far as anyone could tell, I was thriving and happy.

I even started dating a wonderful young man who was also part of the worship team.

The relationship made sense on paper and I thought we seemed well paired. Unfortunately, the young man's mom did not share this sentiment. She did not see me as fit to date her son, and as a young and deeply insecure teenager this was very hurtful. What added to this hurt was that this woman was an extremely influential leader in our church, who I looked up to. I wanted to do the "right" thing make up for whatever badness this woman saw in me but the more I tried the worse things got.

Along the way, I learned the woman had untreated mental illness, a history of physical and sexual abuse, and involvement with the occult. Yet, as a teenager, I did not have the tools to process what was happening.

She spoke down to me often and made me feel like I was less than. She started rumors about me in the church, accusing me of having an inappropriate relationship with her son and of trying to seduce him. She even made up a story about me being "promiscuous" on a mission trip. Not only that but she also accused me of trying to split our church.

Before long, I was receiving ugly anonymous letters and many in the church started treating me differently. She also spoke with other church leaders and convinced them to remove me from my position in the youth group leading worship.

Losing so much of what I found my identity in left me feeling like I was going crazy.

Maybe you are the awful person she says you are.

Maybe you deserve this.

I hoped that leaving for college would bring relief, but early into my freshman year I realized I was severely depressed. Fearing this messy part of me to be inappropriate for who I believed a strong Christian should be, I hid and acted like everything was alright, leading me into even deeper isolation.

I stopped going to church and lost confidence in much of my Christian beliefs. I questioned God and whether he was really there for me. I went looking for comfort instead in synagogues, mosques, and Buddhist temples. I walked away from music entirely - associating it with my pain - and changed my major to world religions, studying the practices of Jainism and Hinduism. I even studied mysticism in Europe for a couple of summers.

Yet none of it seemed to help, and the excruciating ache of loneliness and self-hate took deeper root in my heart. Eventually, all I could feel was numbness.

I spent so many nights sobbing, begging God to show me another way out. Now, in my college dorm room, I am convinced that this is the only escape from my pain.

The accusations scream, capitalizing on the moment: What is wrong with you? Where's your faith? All you think about is yourself. You're disgusting!

Lifting the gun, I press the barrel against my temple.

I slowly squeeze feeling the growing tension of the trigger on my index finger.

It is halfway compressed.

Any moment now.

Without warning, the door of my room opens. I thought I had locked it. I release the trigger and turn to see a friend rush towards me. I put the gun down and burst into tears. They hold me for hours.

Recounting this incident with Pete, even a decade later, left me feeling the weight of these emotions all over again. The visceral pain. The immense loneliness. The memory was difficult to face, but, with Pete's help, I was able to see Jesus in it.

Pete also pointed out that the memory was not the only issue. Jesus also wanted to confront the lies and vows that led me to that moment and also sprouted from that memory.

As we said in the previous section: trauma has the power to shift one's entire perception of reality (our beliefs about God, ourselves, and the world). For me, the mix of past and present traumas were coming together to create a cocktail of lies - internal misbeliefs - and vows - subconscious commitments - that brought me to the cusp of ending my life.

Those thoughts of that night felt so true.

I hated my life.

Hated myself.

> Don't you give up now.
> When it all falls apart
> Let me be the one you lean on when you're not strong enough. Dear daughter, don't let go.
>
> - *Braveheart*

I believed that God and everyone else had abandoned me, and that they probably had a good reason to do so. I was convinced that I was an awful and detestable person, and no matter how much I tried I couldn't change my mind. This is because the lies we believe are immensely powerful and shape how we see everything.

In Genesis, humanity's original rejection of God came about because of an attack on our belief systems.

Now the serpent was more crafty than any of the wild animals the Lord God had made. He said to the woman, "Did God really say, 'You must not eat from any tree in the garden'?"

The woman said to the serpent, "We may eat fruit from the trees in the garden, but God did say, 'You must not eat fruit from the tree that is in the middle of the garden, and you must not touch it, or you will die.'" (Genesis 3:1-3)

The serpent [the spiritual enemy of humanity] says to the first woman, "Did God really say, 'You must not eat from any tree in the garden'?" We see from the very start of the conversation, the woman's understanding of reality is put into question.

Notice the serpent's tactic. He does not challenge the truth directly, but challenges a shade of the truth, reframing what God said ever so slightly. This is because he is not attempting - or able - to change the truth. He instead, in this earliest record of gaslighting, tries to chip away at what the woman believes to be true, challenging her core belief about reality.

We see that the woman initially corrects the serpent, but as the interaction continues it is clear that the woman is in fact questioning what she believes.

"You will not certainly die," the serpent said to the woman. "For God knows that when you eat from it your eyes will be opened, and you will be like God, knowing good and evil." When the woman saw that the fruit of the tree was good for food and pleasing to the eye, and also desirable for gaining wisdom, she took some and ate it. She also gave some to her husband, who was with her, and he ate it. (Genesis 3:4-6)

The serpent now presents a surface level lie ("You will not certainly die") along with a much greater misbelief about who God is and who humanity is. He says, "For God knows that when you eat from it your eyes will be opened, and you will be like God, knowing good and evil."

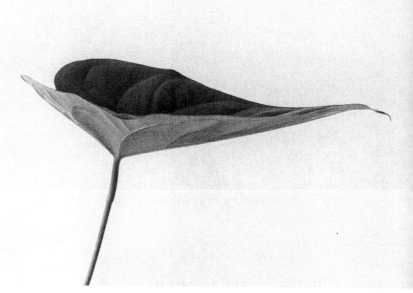

The serpent is effectively challenging whether or not God can be trusted - suggesting that God is not who He presents Himself to be. Furthermore, the deceiver challenges the woman's belief about who she is, saying "you will be like God" only when you eat of this fruit. Yet God had just declared that humanity was made in His image and likeness. (See Gen 1:26)

The serpent is telling the woman she is less than she believes her-

self to be, less than God declares her to be, and the only way to be "more" is through her own pursuit of "God-likeness."

The serpent is able to convince the woman to reject God by assaulting her core beliefs.

It is no wonder that Jesus later calls our spiritual enemy "the father of lies" while pointing out how those who allow his lies to rule in their hearts will inevitably carry out the enemy's desires, which Jesus later identifies as "to steal and kill and destroy." (See Jn 8:44, Jn 10:10)

This is what the enemy desires to do in our hearts. He hopes to capitalize on our trauma and introduce lies into our hearts that will ultimately lead to death and destruction - for ourselves and those around us.

Further complicating the issue are the vows that form from these corrosive lies. Vows are defense mechanisms we develop in the face of trauma in order to cope, survive, or prevent the trauma from repeating.

Psychiatrist and researcher, Dr. Judith Lewis Herman explains that,

> ...repeated trauma in childhood forms and deforms the personality. The child trapped in an abusive environment is faced with formidable tasks of adaptation. She must find a way to preserve a sense of trust in people who are untrustworthy, safety in a situation that is unsafe, control in a situation that is terrifyingly unpredictable, power in a situation of helplessness. Unable to care for or protect herself, she must compensate for the failures of adult care and protection with the only means at her disposal, an immature system of psychological defenses.[1]

These psychological defenses can serve us in moments, but in the long run they are often more harmful than good.

In the story I shared, you see that the vow - *I can't let anyone see the messy parts of me* - actually did me great harm. Though I made that vow at a young age to protect myself from rejection, the enemy

---
[1] Herman, Judith Lewis. Trauma and Recovery: The Aftermath of Violence - From Domestic Abuse to Political Terror. New York, NY: Basic Books, 1992.

used it to further isolate me from the help I needed. Instead of protecting me, this vow was doing the exact opposite.

Jesus' restoration project in me offered an alternative to these lies and the defenses that were no longer helpful. He encouraged in me a renewed understanding of who I was and who He wanted to be for me. Jesus wanted to join me in that memory to show me that He is my protector. He met me in my pain in order to confront on my behalf the lies and vows that developed from my trauma.

Today, recounting this dark time in my life - perhaps the darkest - feels surreal and distant. Those emotions and thoughts feel almost foreign in relation to what Jesus has renewed in me. It is a pivotal part of my story, but the death of it has lost its sting.

Where there was theft, death, and destruction, He gave me truth, grace, and life to the full.

Selah

What might God be highlighting for you in the above section? How have you seen lies impact yours or another's life?

"Braveheart"

My love is safe
It only gives
It doesn't take
So breathe it in
Let it be truth
Where lies have been

Open up your eyes
Darling, lift your head
Dare to take my hand and hold on

Don't you give up now
When it all falls apart
Let me be the one you lean on
When you're not strong enough
Dear daughter
Don't let go

My love is kind
It only heals
It never harms
So breathe it in
Let there be life
Where death has been

Open up your eyes
Darling, lift your head
Dare to take my hand and hold on

Don't you give up now
When it all falls apart
Let me be the one you lean on
When you're not strong enough

Dear daughter
Don't let go
You don't have to hold this

You can let the pieces fall down
I'll be right here with you
To carry you through it all
Dear daughter
Don't let go

Look at how far you've come
And you're still breathing
You've got a brave heart
Such a brave heart
Maybe there's someone out there
Who needs to know that
They've got a brave heart
Such a brave heart
Maybe there's someone out there
Who needs to know that

Don't you give up now
When it all falls apart
Let me be the one you lean on
When you're not strong enough
Dear daughter
Don't let go

You don't have to hold this
You can let the pieces fall down
I'll be right here with you
To carry you through it all
Dear daughter
You've got a brave heart
You've got a brave heart
So don't let go

"I've told you all this so that trusting me, you will be unshakable and assured, deeply at peace. In this godless world you will continue to experience difficulties. But take heart! I've conquered the world."

- Jesus (John 16:33, MSG)

Ripping Open

Without using tools, rip out the next three pages of your book and create something that represents what you are feeling emotionally. Use only the three pages to express to God where you are at this moment. If you feel stuck, consider adding markers or crayons to bring color to your creation. Afterwards journal about the experience and what God showed you through the exercise.

Considering the Impact

Take time to consider some lies you have noticed impacting your life in the past. Ask God to show you how those lies might be impacting your life today.

Stepping Outside of Yourself

Considering one of your wounding memories, imagine consoling the version of you that was wounded in that memory as though they were another person who had been wounded that way. Treat this younger version of yourself with the same kindness and care you would a young person or child whom you love. What would you say to the younger version of yourself? How would you comfort them? What would you say in response to the lies they believe? Afterwards journal about your experience with God.

What would you say to the younger version of yourself?

How would you comfort them?

What would you say in response to the lies they believe?

Journal about your experience with God.

Moving Truth from the Head to the Heart

> But the Lord is faithful, and he will strengthen you and protect you from the evil one.
>
> *- 2 Thessalonians 3:3*

I stand as a child in my gravel driveway. The summer air is muggy and warm, wrapping me with comfort. Wind gently brushes through the lush trees on our land. Birds chirp softly in the distance.

Jesus is here.

We stand face-to-face, His presence brings further comfort. Reaching through skin and bones, I feel Jesus' hands painlessly pass through my chest and wrap around my heart. "I'm your protector, Tasha," He says to me. "Nothing can touch you."

I came back to this God-given vision often, especially while processing the memory of my suicide attempt and the situation surrounding it. It became my *safe place*, an image I could return to when I was feeling overwhelmed or afraid during the healing prayer process. To date, I still return to this picture.

In this vision Jesus also confronted a key lie that was ruling my heart and the powerful vow that grew from it.

The lie: *No one will protect you, Tasha.*

The vow: *I have to protect myself.*

It is important to point out that this lie and vow did not live in my conscious brain as nicely formed sentences, but rather in my unconscious mind as wordless impressions about reality imprinted emotionally on me at a young age and reaffirmed throughout my life. According to Psych Central,[1]

> When the amygdala - the part of the brain believed to play a key role in emotions - becomes aroused, it remains in that state for a long time. At the same time, a memory of the situation becomes imprinted in the brain. The more emotional the situation, the stronger the memory will be. Over time, specific memories become attached to certain emotions.[2]

I experienced situations of extreme emotion where those who were supposed to protect me did not, and my childhood brain was emotionally imprinted by that misbelief. As a result, young Tasha came up with coping strategies designed to build out the protection I felt I lacked. These strategies became my vow.

I have to protect myself.

As I grew older and my conscious mind developed, I knew in my head the Biblical truths that countered that lie and vow. Psalm 18:2 says "The LORD is my rock, my fortress and my deliverer; my God is my rock, in whom I take refuge, my shield and the horn of my salvation, my stronghold."

---

1 Psych Central is an online based organization of psychological professionals dedicated to connecting the general public the help, information, and resources they need.
2 Collingwood, Jane. "How to Beat Negative Thinking." PsychCentral.com. Psych Central, May 17, 2016. https://psychcentral.com/lib/how-to-beat-negative-thinking#1.

However, in the emotion center of my brain - understood as the heart - all the information in the world could not convince me that I was safe to trust others with my protection. I needed God to meet me in that emotion center, to imprint me with a new wordless belief from which would spring a commitment rooted in health and wholeness.

This is what the practices of healing prayer give God permission to do. Our imagination of past memories serves as a psycho-emotional meeting ground, where we are able to open previously guarded places of our heart to God's miraculous healing.

In the previous section, we discussed in depth the ins and outs of reimagining memories with Jesus. The next step of this process is to allow Jesus to speak to you in the context of your memory and imagination.

Once you have identified where Jesus is in your mind's-eye, ask Him what He might have to say to you. Notice not only what He might say, but also what His body language communicates (how is He standing, what is His expression, etc.). Pay particular attention first to what lies and vows He helps you to identify around the memory you are exploring with Him.

Though identifying God's voice is not an exact science and takes practice in discernment, there are some things that can help you to identify what lies and vows Jesus might be pointing out for you.

These misbeliefs and defenses will likely communicate things about God, you, and the world that are counter to what God declares. Though often packaged in palatable ways, ask yourself, *does this belief lead me to greater love for God, myself, and others, or does it lead me to greater death and destruction.*

Also note that vows often arise as statements that begin: *I will always, I will never, I should, or I can't.*

> You knew just how much I hate to wait. Through it you were tender, teaching me to trust. Guess sometimes that's how you grow our faith
>
> *- Thank You For The No*

Once identified, take the time to intentionally lay down and reject those misbeliefs and vows, handing them to Jesus to do with what He will.

Another important part of this process is asking Jesus if there is anyone you need to forgive in or around this memory. This is because unforgiveness can give the lie we are hoping to lay down a continued foothold in our heart. We may need to extend this forgiveness to ourselves for a wound we inflicted on ourselves or others, or even God for a perceived wrong in a given situation.

That said, forgiveness does not mean that you need to reconcile with, reach out to, or ever again have a relationship with the person who has wronged you - and in a situation of severe wounding or abuse, I'd encourage you against such actions.[3]

---

[3] I encourage you to consult a trained therapist or counselor for guidance in processing past abuse.

Forgiveness, rather, simply means that in your heart you are surrendering judgement and justice - the act of making things right - to God. Biblical scholar, Kit Barker writes,

> The victim who forgives is convinced that God will [still] hold the wrongdoer accountable for their sins. God will either count Christ's death as sufficient payment for the sin (if the wrongdoer repents and accepts Christ's death as their own) or, in the absence of penitence, the wrongdoer will, one day, be held accountable for their sin against God... In either case, justice is maintained.[4]

Thus, by surrendering justice to God, you release your offender of any debt they may owe you because of what they have done, trusting that God will deal with them justly.

Keep in mind that though forgiveness is started by our choice to forgive, wounding can be layered and it can take time to allow that forgiveness to work its way through our hearts. Continue to be honest with yourself and God about where you are with forgiving a specific person and continue the practice of forgiveness as you notice areas of unforgiveness in your heart.

Next, ask Jesus if there is any truth He wants to offer you to replace the lie you have believed. Sometimes these truths come in words or a verse from the Bible. Other times they come in feelings of peace, safety, love, courage, etc. Take your time to sit with a potential truth, asking Jesus to affirm if it is for you. Consider what comes to mind and compare it with truth found in scripture. I have often found that these truths Jesus offers me are surprising and something I likely would not have come up with on my own.
The key here is to not be afraid of being wrong, knowing that discerning Jesus' voice takes practice and patience. Remember though, voices that lead you away from love and life, and towards destruction and death, are not from God.

Once you have identified a truth Jesus wants to offer you, take time to intentionally take

---

[4] Barker, Kit. 2016. "Imprecation as Divine Discourse: Speech Act Theory, Dual Authorship, and Theological Interpretation." Journal of Theological Interpretation. Winona Lake, IN: Eisenbrauns.

up and accept this truth in prayer.

The next section will help you to pull this entire process together, but until then keep in mind that our internal belief-systems are a complex combination of physical, emotional, and spiritual hard-wiring. A lifetime of roots cannot be untangled and uprooted in a day. Healing the various parts of our hearts takes time as we learn the rhythm of regularly opening and offering the broken and hidden parts of ourselves to God.

Furthermore, God is wise in his approach with our healing. At times we will not be ready to face a particular memory or lie.

That is okay.

Allow God to lead you in the areas He highlights for you, while being patient with yourself in the areas He is not.

So much of following God is learning to walk at His pace, to not lag behind or push out ahead. In this we avoid approaching our healing as stemming from a religious ritual done in our own strength. Rather Jesus wants us to learn to work at His pace resting when needed and pushing forward when needed.

I'll allow His words in Matthew be the final thought,

> "Are you tired? Worn out? Burned out on religion? Come to me. Get away with me and you'll recover your life. I'll show you how to take a real rest. Walk with me and work with me - watch how I do it. Learn the unforced rhythms of grace. I won't lay anything heavy or ill-fitting on you. Keep company with me and you'll learn to live freely and lightly." (Matthew 11:28-30, MSG)

Selah

Now that you've revisited a memory, acknowledge your emotions surrounding it, and identify the vows that arose from that experience. imagine where Jesus is in the room.

Selah

Spend some time just listening to God, asking Him if there is anything He wants to say or show you in this moment. Allow Him to lead you in living "freely and lightly" as you learn to stay at His pace. Afterwards, journal about your time with God in the space provided.

Creating a Safe Place

Spend some time with God asking Him to help you create a "safe place" in your mind. Slow yourself down, take a few deep breaths, and ask God to bring you to a place of safety. Ask Him to give you an image or vision in your imagination that you can return to when feeling afraid or overwhelmed during this healing prayer process. This should be a place with God that you feel secure and reminded of the truth that God is your protector. It can be a place you know well, a place that you have been only once, or a completely imagined scene. Notice what you are feeling, where God is, and what He says to you in this place. Draw or describe that space below.

"Safe Here"

When I can't catch my breath
Pressed on every side
When all I want is rest
From burdens in this life

Lift up my head
Look me in the eyes and
Tell me I am Yours

I am safe here
Let down my guard
Fall in Your arms
And stay here
I'm not gonna move
Cause when I'm with You

I'm safe
Though I am broken
I know that I am safe
So, so safe here

I don't have to try
I'm never lessly Yours
There's no need to fight
Help me trust You Lord

I am safe here
Let down my guard
Fall in Your arms
And stay here
I'm not gonna move

'Cause when I'm with You
I'm safe
Though I am broken
I know that I am safe
So, so safe

Lift up my head
Look me in the eyes and
Tell me I am Yours

Lift up my head
Look me in the eyes and
Tell me I am Yours
And You are mine
And I am loved

I am safe here
Let down my guard
Fall in Your arms
And stay here
I'm not gonna move
Cause when I'm with You Lord
I'm safe
Though I am broken
I know that I am safe
So, so safe here
Safe here

So, so safe here
Oh, so safe
So safe

I am safe here
So, so safe here

Rest with God

The process of inner healing can be exhausting. It is important to build rest into your regular routine with God. Schedule a time to do something restful with God. You can take a nap, go to a beautiful location, engage in a leisurely activity, or do something mindless and enjoyable. The important thing is to spend time just being with God. When you are done journal about your experience with God.

"Be still, and know
that I am God.
Be still, and know
that I am.
Be still, and know.
Be still.
Be."

- See Psalm 46:10

Trading Lies for Truth

Take some time to practice trading in lies you believe for truths God reveals to you. Ask God for three lies that you have believed/are believing. Feel free to start with some of the more obvious lies that come to mind for you. Write the lies down on the left side of the chart. Next, ask God what truth He wants to reveal to you to replace that lie. Write each truth down on the right side of the chart next to the corresponding lie.

Practice laying down these lies by praying the Prayer of Laying Down (see next page) and crossing out each lie in the left column one by one. Next practice taking up the truths God has revealed to you by praying the Prayer of Taking Up (see next page) and underlining or highlighting each truth in the right column as you do.

Lie	Truth

Prayer of Laying Down

Try praying out loud the following:

Jesus, in Your name and by Your power, I lay down and reject the lie (insert lie) and the vow (insert vow) that springs from it. I surrender these to You to do with what You will. Amen.

Try reciting this prayer with your hands upward in your lap, imagining Jesus lifting the lie and vow from your hands.

Prayer of Taking Up

Try praying out loud the following:

Jesus, in Your name and by Your power, I accept and take up the truth that insert truth. I open my hands and heart to You and this gift You offer me. Thank You for Your truth. Amen.

Try reciting this prayer with your hands upward in your lap, imagining Jesus laying a gift into your hands.

PART 4

BRINGING IT ALL TOGETHER

The few years following my healing prayer intensive with Pete were nothing short of incredible. I felt happier with who I was - who God had made me to be. I noticed that I was friendlier to strangers, more patient with friends and family, and, above all, kinder to myself.

I felt the lies of my childhood draining away as I regularly employed in my everyday life the prayer practices I learned while in Colorado. I never truly believed I could feel this sort of freedom. Now, after all the years of waiting, hoping, and yearning, I was starting to taste the abundant life I had only heard of since I was a child. Not long after my journey with healing prayer, I met the man who would become my husband, Keith. He was handsome, kind, and so encouraging of who God had created me to be.

A little over a year later we were engaged.

It was not long into our marriage that we started considering children. Keith had been open with me that for about ten years he had known it was unlikely that he would ever be able to conceive naturally. He had been told it was most likely due to a back injury

as a teenager - one that was still causing him chronic pain.

As we were exploring alternative options, I heard God say to me one day, "It will be a sign to Keith." I felt like God was inviting us to start praying to have a baby naturally, something that would take a great deal of trust.

Knowing that Keith had worked through so much grief around this topic already, I was nervous to share with him what I had heard God say. I didn't want him to hope again and have to go through that disappointment again. Despite my fear, I stepped out in faith sharing what I believed I heard.

Keith took some time to listen to God too and discern alongside me. Despite some skepticism, Keith and I both began to pray, calling on God to give us the miraculous gift of a child.

While we were on a mission trip in Uganda, God answered.

During a time of worship and prayer with our team, I was leading the song *Miracles* by Jesus Culture. Out of the corner of my eye, I see Keith on the ground crying. I knew something was up.

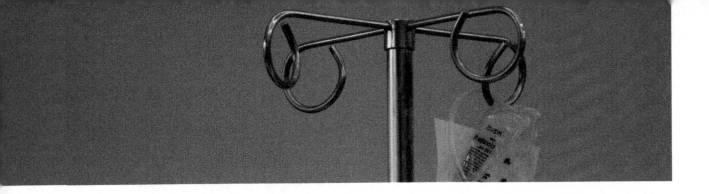

Soon after seeing him that way, Keith stopped me in the middle of worship and whispered in my ear, "I think God just healed my back."

"What do you mean?" I whispered back.

"I'm warm all over and I can't get it to hurt."

We reported this to the rest of the team and we all praised God. That was the first of many physical healings that night and Keith hasn't had back problems since. That night, the team prayed for us to be able to have a baby.

Two months later, we were pregnant with our son, Levi.

My faith had never been stronger. As we began to pray for health and ease in regards to our son's birth, I knew in my heart God would faithfully answer these requests. I was shocked when things did not turn out the way I had believed they would.

When the time came for Levi's birth, not only was I in horribly painful labor for over thirty-three hours and lost a lot of blood, it seemed like so many things that could've gone wrong, did.

And when Levi finally arrived, he came out not breathing. Panicked moments ensued as I, a dizzied new mom, helplessly watched my blue breathless baby cling to his brand new life.

Thankfully he was resuscitated, but he ended up being in the NICU for over a week and we weren't sure if there was going to be any long term damage to Levi's body

> So would You hold on to these burdens 'Cause they weigh me down, and I wanna run with You.
>
> *- Love Lifting Me*

or brain.

And the difficulty did not stop there. My recovery was brutal and even required surgery two weeks after my delivery - while Keith was gone on a trip for work! The postpartum effects on my body led to overwhelming anxiety and depression. I couldn't even go to the grocery store without having a panic attack.

The sleep deprivation that comes with being a new mom didn't help the matter either. I felt isolated again - deeply lonely in the struggle.

It seemed like anything I prayed for, the opposite would happen.
Remembering the words of a friend - anxiety and depression are just the body's way of telling you something needs to change - I leaned in to these feelings asking God for help:

What is going on God?

Where are you?

Are you trying to teach me something?

As these questions were met with silence and the difficulties of my recovery continued, I stopped praying without even realizing it. It was not until a year after giving birth, that I noticed how much my

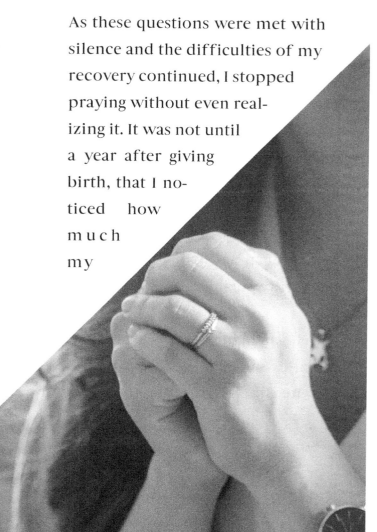

spiritual life had suffered - how discouraged I was when talking to God.

In a moment of grace-given courage, I pulled out the photos taken the day of the delivery - photos I had never been able to look at. The emotions of that memory were deep and painful, the trauma still palpable.

I felt a nudging in my heart - God's gentle touch encouraging me to invite Him into this memory.

Returning to the healing prayer practices I had learned with Pete in Colorado, Jesus showed me where He was during my delivery: next to me the whole time, protecting my life, protecting my son. He revealed to me the lie that had been seeded in my heart as a result of the trauma of my delivery.
You betrayed me, Jesus. You abandoned me.

For over a year, my embarrassment and pride had blinded me of this lie. Afterall, Jesus and I had history. I was no rookie in the faith. I was mad at myself for allowing such a lie to creep back into my heart. I thought I had this following Jesus thing figured out.

Now Jesus, in His gentle and kind way, was again meeting me at the point of my trauma. With far more grace than I was giving myself, He was showing me how much more

I had to grow.

That is the strange part of this process of internal healing: the more you are grown by God, the more aware you become of how much greater growth is needed. That is why continued humility is an essential part of this ongoing inner healing process.

Humility is not, as many believe, seeing yourself as less than.

Rather it is simply seeing yourself clearly.

Humility celebrates the growth that has already come, while still recognizing the growth that is yet to be. It understands a person's identity as a child of God, while taking seriously the desperate need of God's continued deliverance and transformation.

Reimagining my delivery through healing prayer, Jesus gently drew my attention to this lack of humility. "I have you, Tasha. You can trust me," He said compassionately. "And you know what, I have Levi too." This truth cut deeply and gently to the core of my heart.

Trust in the Lord with all your heart and lean not on your own understanding; in all your ways submit to him, and he will make your paths straight.
- Proverbs 3:5-6

I saw myself with such clarity in that moment.

I saw that I was trying to control every outcome of my delivery. My trust was not in God, but in my ability to manage God. I thought that God couldn't respond to my prayer with a "no." I believed that I knew better than God what was best for me and my baby.

Though I had grown so much, there were still so many areas of my heart that still needed His attention.

Despite the power of going through this process with God around the memory of Levi's birth, I still found a great deal of fear present when God allowed us to become pregnant with our second child, Lyla.

I was afraid of another long and painful labor. I was afraid that she would come out not breathing.
I knew that God wanted to bring me to an even greater level of healing. He wanted to use the very same type of situation in which the trauma was caused to bring

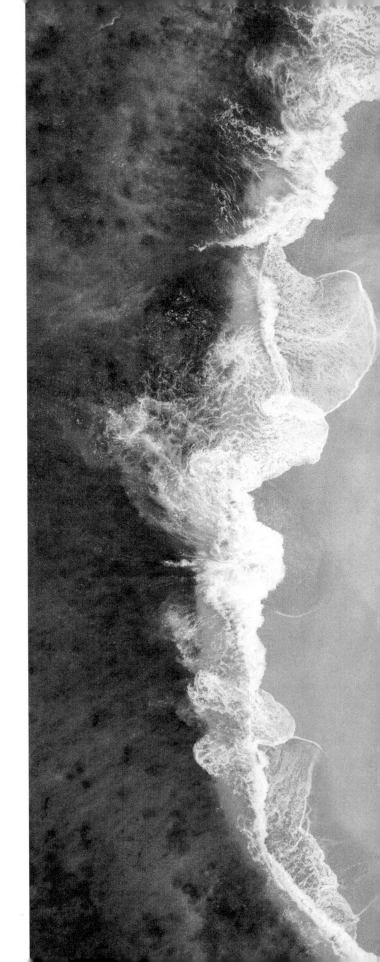

healing to me in that area.

I was reminded of the story of Jesus healing the blind man in Mark 8, that says,

He took the blind man by the hand and led him outside the village. When he had spit on the man's eyes and put his hands on him, Jesus asked, "Do you see anything?" He looked up and said, "I see people; they look like trees walking around."

> *Once more Jesus put his hands on the man's eyes. Then his eyes were opened, his sight was restored, and he saw everything clearly. (Mark 8:23-25)*

Jesus shows in this story that healing is often a process. At times we need to grow in one area just to be able to see the growth needed in another.

Seeing this was the case for me, I walked through the healing prayer process again, returning to the memory of Levi's birth with Jesus. I allowed Him to further mend my wounded heart and, as a result, I was able to approach my daughter's delivery with trust that no matter what happened God was in control. He had me and He had Lyla. He was our protector.

And when Lyla was born naturally and quickly, healthy and breathing, all I could do was cry out in all

sincerity, "Thank you, God! Thank you!"

As we venture into this final section together, keep in mind that what you find in these pages is only scaffolding - a splinting wire mesh around a young plant. It is for guiding your growth as you learn to rely on God, learn the unique look of His specialized relationship with you.

It is sometimes tempting to believe that we can use a specific method of prayer or religious practice to control outcomes in our lives. This method of healing prayer is no different. It - like anything - can become an idol, a means of control and manipulation in our relationship with God.

It will serve us well in these moments to remember that the real power of healing comes from not a practice but a person.

The person of Jesus.

He is the only one who is powerful enough to break the chains of the lies that bound us. He is the only one who can move truth down into the depths of our hearts.

Selah

Where might you be relying on your own strength rather than Gods? Ask God to reveal to you blind spots in your heart that you may be overlooking. Record your prayer in the journaling space below.

"Therefore, my dear friends, as you have always obeyed not only in my presence, but now much more in my absence continue to work out your salvation with fear and trembling, for it is God who works in you to will and to act in order to fulfill his good purpose."

- Philippians 2:12-13

Truths to Hold to

Take some time to prayerfully consider with God the truths that He wants you to hold onto in regards to yourself, Him, and the world around you. Record these truths in the appropriate section of the Venn diagram below, noting the truths that may intersect with two or all three categories.

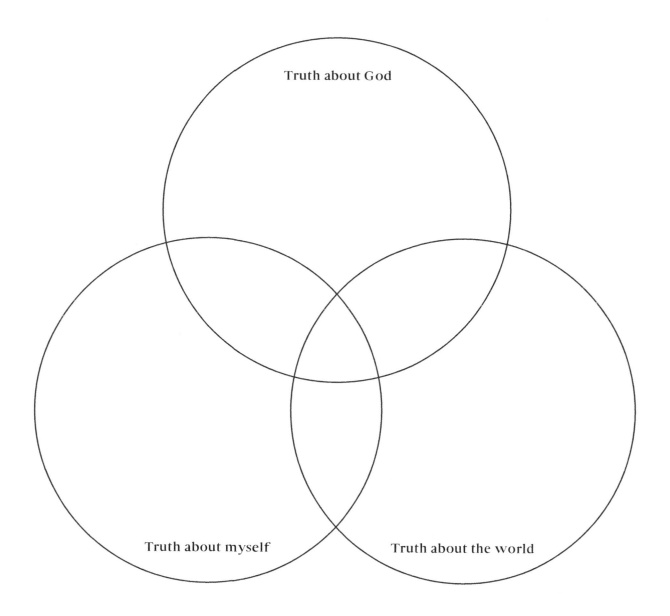

Practicing Imaginative Prayer with Scripture

Part of the healing process is learning to allow God to speak to you through your imagination. Though He can speak through the reimagining of our memories, He can also speak through our imagining of stories in scripture. Enter into the following passage of scripture using your imagination to put yourself in the place of Martha. Pause after each line to imagine yourself in the situation. First imagine your physical sensations (what you see, smell, hear, etc.). Next, imagine how you feel (towards the situation, your sister Mary, towards Jesus). Finally, ask Jesus what He is telling you through the passage. Afterwards, journal about your experience.

As Jesus and the disciples continued on their way to Jerusalem, they came to a certain village where a woman named Martha welcomed Him into her home.

Her sister, Mary, sat at the Lord's feet, listening to what He taught. But Martha was distracted by the big dinner she was preparing.

She came to Jesus and said, "Lord, doesn't it seem unfair to you that my sister just sits here while I do all the work? Tell her to come and help me."

But the Lord said to her, "My dear Martha, you are worried and upset over all these details!

There is only one thing worth being concerned about. Mary has discovered it, and it will not be taken away from her."

Luke 10:38-42

Looking at the Whole Process

Over the next few pages I've tried to lay out in detail how to practically engage in the healing prayer process. This is meant to be a flexible structure that bends and stretches depending on what you need and what God is doing. Hold the flow and order loosely and continually open your heart to what God is up to.

There will be times that you follow this journal structure closely. And other times God will lead you to lay aside this structure for the sake of what He is doing in a given moment.

Don't mishear me. Each step is important and avoiding elements of this process because of fear or discomfort will work against your healing.

I am simply encouraging you to allow your discernment of God to grow as He leads you beyond this scaffolding and into the nuance and adaptation that comes with any healthy relationship.

Process Pages

In the following section of the journal you will be provided with process pages (see the sample below). Each process page is designed to guide you step-by-step through the healing prayer process for a specific memory.

Be conscious of when you plan to engage in this process as it can often be emotionally and spiritually draining. Though you may find extended time while on a retreat or at a weekend away, I generally suggest engaging with only one memory in a given sitting, and providing yourself plenty of time afterwards to decompress.

The sections below describe each element of the process page in more detail.

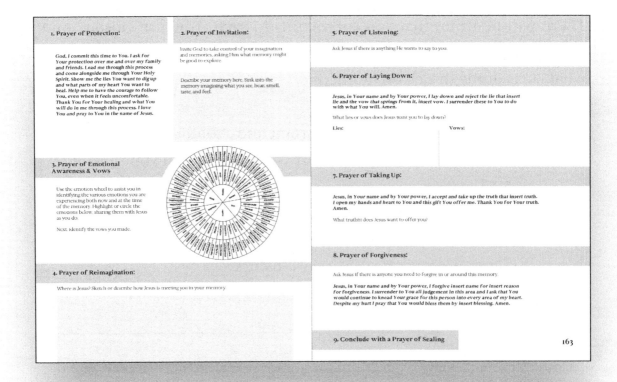

One: Prayer of Protection

Before you begin, I encourage you to return to the prayer of protection found in the first section of this journal. Simply ask God to protect you and those close to you during and after this prayer time. As a reminder this prayer can look something like this:

God, I commit this time to You. I ask for Your protection over me and over my family and friends. Lead me through this process and come alongside me through Your Holy Spirit. Show me the lies You want to dig up and what parts of my heart You want to heal. Help me to have the courage to follow You, even when it feels uncomfortable. Thank You for Your healing and what You will do in me through this process. I love You and pray to You in the name of Jesus.

In the space below, feel free to write out your own version of the prayer of protection, adapting the lines above into your own words that flow more naturally.

Two: Prayer of Invitation

Next, spend a moment inviting God to take control of your imagination and memories. Consider what you would like to bring to Jesus during this time and what memory might be good for you to process together. Ask God if He has an opinion about what memory you both might explore. Invite God to speak to you through this memory and recognize His presence in this sacred space with you. This is a reminder that you are surrendering control here to God and His will, trusting that He will lead you where you need to go.

If you are having trouble locking on to one specific memory, reference your timeline from part one for inspiration.

Use the space provided on the process page to really flesh out this memory, describing the scene in detail and considering your senses - what you see, hear, smell, feel, and taste.

Once you have recorded the details of the memory on the process page, allow God to help you really sink into the memory in your imagination.

If things begin to feel overwhelming, gently return to the "safe place" in your mind that you and God set up in the previous section. Remind yourself of the words God offered you during this safe space exercise.

Selah

Before moving on to the rest of the reading, take some time to write out what God might be highlighting for you in this section so far.

Three: Prayer of Emotional Awareness & Vows

Also prayerfully consider what you were feeling emotionally at the time the memory took place, and what you are feeling emotionally now as someone re-imagining that memory with God. Use the emotion wheel on your process page to assist you in identifying the various emotions you are experiencing. Highlight or circle the emotions that best describe what you are feeling. Take some time to just tell Jesus about these various emotions, sharing with Him openly and honestly.

Now that you have identified your emotions, next you will want to ask Jesus what lies and/or vows He wants you to confront in this memory and lay down. Remember, vows are unconscious commitments we make in response to the lies we believe, often arising as statements that begin: I will always, I will never, I should, or I can't.

For example, if I believe that I am not worth loving, I may unconsciously vow to not allow myself to grow close in relationship to another person so as not to be rejected.

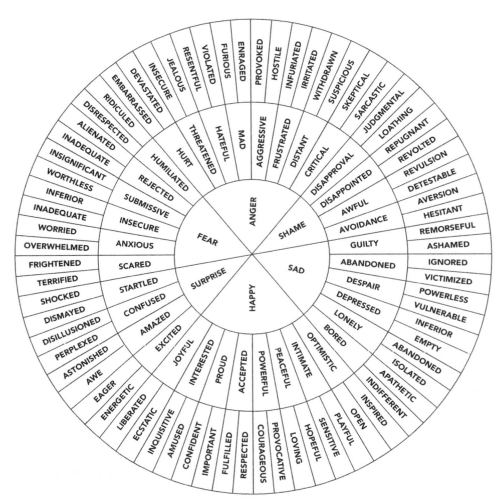

Four: Prayer of Reimagination

Once you are well acquainted with the memory, ask God to show you where Jesus is in the midst of this memory. Take your time and really discern what He wants to show you.

Once you identify where Jesus is, consider what you notice about how He is meeting you in the scene.

Where is He? What is His expression? What does His body language communicate? How do you feel in His presence?

In the space provided on the process page sketch or describe how Jesus is meeting you.

Five: Prayer of Listening

Now, ask Jesus if there is anything He wants to tell you in this moment. Spend some time just listening and discerning what He might want to say to you, remembering that Jesus' voice is one of love and life.

Tell Him the emotions you felt/feel and ask Him what He wants to tell you surrounding those.

Record what He has to say in the space provided to you on the process page.

Six: Prayer of Laying Down

Next you will want to ask Jesus what lies and/or vows He wants you to confront in this memory and lay down. Remember, vows are unconscious commitments we make in response to the lies we believe, often arising as statements that begin: *I will always, I will never, I should, or I can't.*

For example, if I believe that I am not worth loving, I may unconsciously vow to not allow myself to grow close in relationship to another person so as not to be rejected.

Once you have identified these, write them in the space provided on your process page. Spend some time, then, intentionally laying these lies and vows down to Jesus in prayer.
You can try reciting the following prayer out loud, with your hands upward in your lap. As you do imagine Jesus lifting the lies and vows from your hands, and doing with them what he will.

Jesus, in Your name and by Your power, I lay down and reject the lie that <u>insert lie</u> and the vow that springs from it, <u>insert vow</u>. I surrender these to You to do with what You will. Amen.

Afterwards ask Jesus if there is anything more He would like to tell you or reveal to you. If He reveals to you additional lies and vows, offer those to Him in the same way you did before, praying the prayer of laying down with your hands up before you. Also, consider what you might want to say in response to what Jesus reveals.

Seven: Prayer of Taking Up

In the same way that you have laid down the lies and vows of a given memory, ask Jesus what truth He wants to offer you in place of these lies and vows.

This can be a correction of a misbelief about yourself, God, or the world. These may come as general impressions or as words or phrases from God, such as: *You are enough for Me, what happened to you is not your fault, you can be healed, I love you as My son/daughter, etc.*

Once you have identified the truth or truths Jesus wants to offer you, record them in the space provided on your process page. Recite the following prayer with your hands in the same position, upward in your lap. This time, imagine Jesus instead offering you the truth He has revealed to you as a gift, placing it into your hands.

Jesus, in Your name and by Your power, I accept and take up the truth that insert truth. *I open my hands and heart to You and this gift You offer me. Thank You for Your truth. Amen.*

Eight: Prayer of Forgiveness

Forgiveness is a huge part of the healing process. Remember, forgiveness does not mean that you need to find a way to again have a relationship with the person you are forgiving. This sort of reconciliation is especially advised against in the case of severe wounding or abuse.

In forgiving we are simply surrendering justice and judgement to God.

Another powerful step in forgiveness is allowing yourself to "love your enemies and pray for those who persecute you." (Mt 5:44) This can start simply by declaring a blessing over the wronging party, asking God to bring about a specific good in their life - however small. This simple yet powerful act of praying blessing for those who do not necessarily deserve it, can make a massive difference in freeing us from unforgiveness in our hearts.

Once you have identified those Jesus is calling you to forgive in or around a given memory, pray the following prayer aloud, focusing on surrendering judgment and justice to Him.

Jesus, in Your name and by Your power, I forgive <u>insert name</u> for <u>insert reason for forgiveness</u>. I surrender to You all judgement and justice in this area and ask that You would continue to knead Your grace for this person into every area of my heart. Despite my hurt, I pray that You would bless them by <u>insert blessing</u>. Amen.

Nine: Prayer of Sealing

The final stage of this process is to ask God to seal in your heart the truth He has given you during this time of prayer.

This prayer of sealing can look something like this:

God, thank You for relieving me of the burden these lies and vows have placed on my heart. By the name and power of Jesus, seal these out of my heart and inner beliefs. I thank You also for the gift of truth that You have given me during this time of prayer. By the name and power of Jesus, seal this truth inside of my heart and inner beliefs, that I may believe what is true about You, myself, and the world, and that I may live from that truth in my life. I love You, Lord. Amen.

Afterwards, take some time to collect yourself by taking a few deep breaths. Consider engaging in something restful with God.

Selah

As you prepare to bring all these healing prayer practices together with God, talk to Him truthfully about how you are feeling. Remember that emotions are just indicators of what is going on at a deeper level in our hearts. Ask God what He wants to reveal to you with these emotions.

"being confident of this, that he who began a good work in you will carry it on to completion until the day of Christ Jesus."

- Philippians 1:6

Some Final Thoughts

I am so honored to have been able to share with you the pieces of my story found in these pages. I pray that they introduce you to a world of prayer and connection with God, that far surpasses anything I could have ever offered you.

Know that this journal is merely an invitation into the practices of healing prayer and what God might offer you through them. God has introduced me to so much more than I am able to share with you in this journal, and my hope has always been that He would take what you have started here and multiply it beyond what you or I could ever imagine.

I encourage you, then, to keep exploring.

I pray that these practices of surrender and humility become so ingrained into your life that they become a hallmark of your relationship with Jesus - a natural outpouring of openness, vulnerability, and trust.

Through that outpouring you will find that Jesus is restoring your heart - returning you to Eden and to who you were always meant to be.

A loved child.

Free.

Boundless.

Releasing the Lies

As a prophetic act of release, take the lies that come up while going through your process pages with God and write them on some small stones. Taking those stones to a lake, river, or ocean, throw them into the water as a prophetic act of releasing them for good. Feel free to be creative, considering other prophetic acts instead of this one that can symbolize your release of these lies. Afterwards, thank God for His healing. Journal your reflections on the experience in the space provided.

Looking Back at Your Letter

In the first section of this book, you wrote a letter to God telling Him about what you hope engaging with Him through this journal might bring. Look back at that letter with God and thank Him for the healing and growth you have seen over the course of this journal. Share with Him where you are still hoping to grow. Ask God how He would like to affirm you after working through this journal. Record your prayer time in the journaling pages below.

"He will wipe every tear from their eyes. There will be no more death' or mourning or crying or pain, for the old order of things has passed away."

- Revelation 21:4

Process Page

1. Prayer of Protection:

God, I commit this time to You. I ask for Your protection over me and over my family and friends. Lead me through this process and come alongside me through Your Holy Spirit. Show me the lies You want to dig up and what parts of my heart You want to heal. Help me to have the courage to follow You, even when it feels uncomfortable. Thank You for Your healing and what You will do in me through this process. I love You and pray to You in the name of Jesus.

2. Prayer of Invitation:

Invite God to take control of your imagination and memories, asking Him what memory might be good to explore.

Describe your memory here. Sink into the memory imagining what you see, hear, smell, taste, and feel.

3. Prayer of Emotional Awareness & Vows

Use the emotion wheel to assist you in identifying the various emotions you are experiencing both now and at the time of the memory. Highlight or circle the emotions below, sharing them with Jesus as you do.

Next, identify the vows you made.

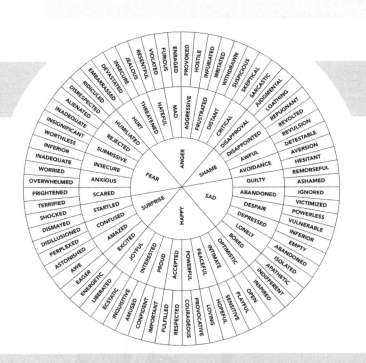

4. Prayer of Reimagination:

Where is Jesus? Sketch or describe how Jesus is meeting you in your memory.

5. Prayer of Listening:

Ask Jesus if there is anything He wants to say to you.

6. Prayer of Laying Down:

Jesus, in Your name and by Your power, I lay down and reject the lie that insert lie and the vow that springs from it, insert vow. I surrender these to You to do with what You will. Amen.

What lies or vows does Jesus want you to lay down?

Lies: Vows:

7. Prayer of Taking Up:

Jesus, in Your name and by Your power, I accept and take up the truth that insert truth. I open my hands and heart to You and this gift You offer me. Thank You for Your truth. Amen.

What truth(s) does Jesus want to offer you?

8. Prayer of Forgiveness:

Ask Jesus if there is anyone you need to forgive in or around this memory.

Jesus, in Your name and by Your power, I forgive insert name for insert reason for forgiveness. I surrender to You all judgement in this area and I ask that You would continue to knead Your grace for this person into every area of my heart. Despite my hurt I pray that You would bless them by insert blessing. Amen.

9. Conclude with a Prayer of Sealing

Made in the USA
Middletown, DE
23 April 2022